Gourmet Vitamix Blender Soup Recipes

Get The Most Out of Your Vitamix Blender With These Amazing, Delicious, Quick and Easy Recipes

By: Vanessa Lee

Disclaimer and Terms of Use:

Table of Contents

Introduction

The Vitamix blender is one of the best blenders available on the market today, and these recipes are perfect for the blender with its innovative features. These soup recipes are easy to make and give you another option for fast and quick meals outside of the normal smoothies that you might make with the blender. T

The Vitamix is a unique blender because it can be used to make complicated soup recipes that would otherwise take you several minutes to chop up each ingredient. Soups that may otherwise take 50 to 60 minutes to prepare by hand can be made in just 20 minutes with the Vitamix blender, and if you aren't using your Vitamix to make soups you are missing out on one of its best features and capabilities.

Vitamix blenders are one of the top blenders available anywhere, and the versatility of the Vitamix is virtually unparalleled. The blender comes with a heavy duty motor that can handle just about any veggie or ingredient that you might use for a soup. Vitamix blenders are particularly well suited for making soups because they can break down fibrous vegetables quite easily, and the quality and consistency of the soups that you will get out of this blender will be amazing. Keep in mind that many of these recipes call for you to move ladles of hot soup into the blender to puree, so be sure to use caution and you should allow the soup to cool slightly before you ladle and blend it.

This report contains a wide range of different soups that you can use with a Vitamix blender, and these soups are designed to be easy to make with the blender. Most of these recipes take just 15 to 20 minutes to prepare, and you can have a hearty and delicious meal with these soup options. These soups are specifically intended for the Vitamix blender because they may contain ingredients that are otherwise difficult for other blenders to break down.

These recipes are intended for use with any Vitamix blender model. Some models like the Professional version have a puree program that you can use to puree the ingredients, but if you have a standard Vitamix model you can follow the instructions in this recipe book to puree ingredients using variable setting 1-10. There are a wide variety of different recipes included in this guide so that you have several options available, and there are also both hot and cold recipes included.

Most of these recipes are very healthy, but one thing to consider is that vegetable stock or chicken stock is often high sodium, so you may want to replace it with low sodium stock or even homemade vegetable stock if you are concerned at all about sodium intake.

The Vitamix is unique simply because of its power and durability, and these soups will in no way harm the blender or wear it down so you can repeat them as many times as you want. I hope you enjoy these recipes and that this guide serves you well whenever you need a quick meal or a great side dish idea.

Vitamix Tomato Soup

If you need a simple tomato soup, this one is perfect and doesn't take very much time to make at all.

Ingredients:

- 1 tbsp. olive oil
- 1 tbsp. butter
- 1 onion, chopped
- 1 celery stalk, chopped
- 1 tsp. thyme, chopped
- 4 cups chicken broth
- 3 cans peeled tomatoes, whole with juice (about 14 oz. each)
- 3 cloves garlic, minced
- Salt and pepper to taste

Directions:

1. Heat oil and butter in a Dutch oven on medium until butter starts to melt.
2. Add celery and onion and cook until softened, about 6 minutes.
3. Add thyme and garlic and cook for about 30 seconds.
4. Add canned tomatoes and juice and chicken broth and bring to a boil.
5. Reduce heat to low and simmer uncovered for 10 minutes.
6. Add soup to Vitamix blender, select Setting 1.
7. Slowly increase speed to 10 and then High.
8. Blend 3-4 minutes or longer until mixture is fully pureed.
9. Season with salt and pepper and serve.

Servings: 8
Calories per Serving: 86

Nutrition Facts

Serving Size 290 g

Amount Per Serving

Calories 86   Calories from Fat 40

% Daily Value*

Total Fat 4.4g	**7%**
Saturated Fat 1.4g	**7%**
Trans Fat 0.0g	
Cholesterol 4mg	**1%**
Sodium 408mg	**17%**
Potassium 465mg	**13%**
Total Carbohydrates 9.2g	**3%**
Dietary Fiber 2.0g	**8%**
Sugars 1.0g	
Protein 3.9g	

Vitamin A 20%	•	Vitamin C 67%
Calcium 2%	•	Iron 6%

Nutrition Grade A

* Based on a 2000 calorie diet

Vitamix Black Bean Soup

This very interesting black bean soup recipe is delicious and hearty, and it goes very well with rice, a quesadilla or a sandwich.

Ingredients:

- 1 cup chicken broth
- ½ tsp. cumin
- ½ tsp. green tabasco sauce
- 2 tsp. chili powder
- 3 garlic cloves, minced
- ½ onion, minced
- 1 tbsp. olive oil

- 1 ½ cup water
- 2 cans black beans, drained
- Salt and pepper to taste
- Sour cream, salsa and cilantro for garnish.

Directions:

1. Heat oil in a large saucepan on medium.
2. Add onion and sauté until softened, about 8 to 9 minutes.
3. Add garlic and sauté for another minute.
4. And cumin, chili powder, salt and pepper to taste and sauté for 30 seconds.
5. Add water, beans, and chicken broth and bring to a boil.
6. Lower heat, cover and simmer 15 minutes.
7. Add 2 ladles of soup into the Vitamix blender, select Setting 1.
8. Slowly increase speed to 10 and then High.
9. Blend 3-4 minutes or longer until mixture is fully pureed.
10. Re-add the blended soup back into the pot and season with hot sauce and stir.
11. Portion in soup bowls and add sour cream, cilantro and salsa as desired and serve.

Servings: 4
Calories per Serving: 384

Nutrition Facts

Serving Size 267 g

Amount Per Serving

Calories 384   Calories from Fat 50

% Daily Value*

Total Fat 5.5g	**8%**
Saturated Fat 1.0g	**5%**
Cholesterol 0mg	**0%**
Sodium 213mg	**9%**
Potassium 1550mg	**44%**
Total Carbohydrates 63.6g	**21%**
Dietary Fiber 15.6g	**62%**
Sugars 2.9g	
Protein 22.7g	

Vitamin A 8%	•	Vitamin C 4%
Calcium 14%	•	Iron 30%

Nutrition Grade A

* Based on a 2000 calorie diet

Vitamix Leek-Potato Bisque

This is delicious and rich potato-leek bisque that turns out to be very cream but doesn't even have cream as an ingredient.

Ingredients:

- 1 tbsp. olive oil
- 1.5 pounds of leeks, sliced (green and white part only)
- 0.75 pounds potatoes, diced and peeled
- 1.5 cups low fat milk
- 1 cup chicken broth
- 1.5 tbsp. lemon juice
- ¼ tsp. white pepper
- 1 tsp. salt

Directions:

1. Heat olive oil in a large soup pot (Dutch oven) on medium.
2. Add ½ tsp. salt and leeks and cook until tender, about 25 minutes.
3. Add water to prevent sticking.
4. Add milk, chicken broth and diced potatoes to the pot.
5. Bring to a simmer cover and cook about 15 minutes until potatoes are tender.
6. Remove from heat and add soup into Vitamix blender with a ladle, select Setting 1.
7. Slowly increase speed to 10 and then High.
8. Blend 3-4 minutes or longer until mixture is fully pureed.
9. Add pureed soup to bowls and season with white pepper, salt and lemon juice and serve.

Servings: 4
Calories per Serving: 242

Nutrition Facts

Serving Size 418 g

Amount Per Serving

Calories 242   Calories from Fat 48

% Daily Value*

Total Fat 5.4g	**8%**
Saturated Fat 1.3g	**7%**
Cholesterol 5mg	**2%**
Sodium 853mg	**36%**
Potassium 850mg	**24%**
Total Carbohydrates 42.4g	**14%**
Dietary Fiber 5.1g	**21%**
Sugars 12.7g	
Protein 8.3g	

Vitamin A 60%	•	Vitamin C 66%
Calcium 22%	•	Iron 23%

Nutrition Grade A

* Based on a 2000 calorie diet

Vitamix Broccoli Soup

This is a low calorie simple and delicious broccoli soup that doesn't take much time to prepare and includes delicious olive oil, butter and garlic for a hearty and rich flavor.

Ingredients:

- 4 cups broccoli, chopped (stems and florets)
- ½ tsp. salt
- ½ tbsp. butter
- ½ onion, chopped
- ½ celery stalk, chopped
- ½ tsp. fresh parsley or thyme
- 1 cup water
- 2 cups chicken broth
- ¼ cup half and half
- 2 cloves garlic, minced
- Pepper to taste

Directions:

1. Heat oil and butter in a large soup pot (Dutch oven) on medium until butter starts to melt
2. Add celery and onion and cook for about 7 minutes until softened.
3. Add parsley and garlic and cook for about 30 seconds.
4. Add broccoli, broth and water and bring to a boil on high.
5. Reduce and simmer and cook until tender, about 5 to 6 minutes.
6. Add half and half into soup and season with salt.
7. Add soup to Vitamix blender with a ladle, select Setting 1.
8. Slowly increase speed to 10 and then High.
9. Blend 3-4 minutes or longer until mixture is fully pureed.
10. Portion into bowls, season pureed soup with pepper and serve.

Servings: 4
Calories per Serving: 91

Nutrition Facts

Serving Size 305 g

Amount Per Serving

Calories 91   Calories from Fat 38

% Daily Value*

Total Fat 4.2g	**6%**
Saturated Fat 2.2g	**11%**
Trans Fat 0.0g	
Cholesterol 9mg	**3%**
Sodium 723mg	**30%**
Potassium 445mg	**13%**
Total Carbohydrates 9.0g	**3%**
Dietary Fiber 2.7g	**11%**
Sugars 2.5g	
Protein 5.7g	

Vitamin A 14%	•	Vitamin C 138%
Calcium 7%	•	Iron 6%

Nutrition Grade A

* Based on a 2000 calorie diet

Vitamix Cauliflower Cheese Soup

If you need a delicious and filling soup and you're a fan of cauliflower you can't go wrong with this one.

Ingredients:

- 1 head of cauliflower, chopped
- ½ cup Monterey jack cheese, shredded
- ¼ tsp. Spanish paprika (or regular)
- ½ cup cheddar cheese
- 3 tbsp. all-purpose flour
- 1 onion soup mix package
- 1 cup low fat milk
- Salt and pepper to taste

Directions:

1. Add onion soup mix and cauliflower into a Dutch oven or soup pot and add just enough cold water to cover the cauliflower.
2. Heat on high until boiling them reduce heat to low and simmer uncovered for 10 minutes until cauliflower is softened.
3. Add butter, flour and milk into pot and stir.
4. Ladle cauliflower and soup mixture into Vita-mix blender and select Setting 1.
5. Slowly increase speed to 10 and then High.
6. Blend 3-4 minutes or longer until mixture is fully pureed.
7. Put blended soup back into soup pot and add cheeses and stir well.
8. Add paprika and salt and pepper to taste.
9. Add more water to thin soup if necessary and simmer for 6 minutes.
10. Allow to cool and serve.

Servings: 4
Calories per Serving: 173

Nutrition Facts

Serving Size 161 g

Amount Per Serving

Calories 173   Calories from Fat 87

% Daily Value*

Total Fat 9.7g	**15%**
Saturated Fat 6.1g	**30%**
Cholesterol 30mg	**10%**
Sodium 210mg	**9%**
Potassium 324mg	**9%**
Total Carbohydrates 11.3g	**4%**
Dietary Fiber 1.8g	**7%**
Sugars 4.9g	
Protein 11.0g	

Vitamin A 8%	•	Vitamin C 51%
Calcium 30%	•	Iron 4%

Nutrition Grade B

* Based on a 2000 calorie diet

Vitamix Zucchini Soup

This zucchini soup is one of the easier Vitamix soups and it is a must-try for zucchini fans.

Ingredients:

- 8 zucchini, sliced
- 1 onion, chopped
- 3 garlic cloves, minced
- 4 cups vegetable stock
- 4 tsp. cumin
- 1 tsp. black pepper
- 1 tsp. ground cardamom
- ½ tsp. cayenne pepper
- 1 tbsp. olive oil

Directions:

1. Sauté garlic, onions, and zucchini in a pan with olive oil on medium.
2. Add 1 can of broth after about 6 minutes and all spices and continue cooking until tender but still slightly firm.
3. Ladle soup into Vitamix, select Puree setting and puree.
4. Stop blending once soup is thickened and almost completely pureed.
5. Serve in bowls.

Servings: 4
Calories per Serving: 166

Nutrition Facts

Serving Size 725 g

Amount Per Serving

Calories 166   Calories from Fat 59

% Daily Value*

Total Fat 6.5g	**10%**
Saturated Fat 1.2g	**6%**
Cholesterol 0mg	**0%**
Sodium 987mg	**41%**
Potassium 1386mg	**40%**
Total Carbohydrates 19.3g	**6%**
Dietary Fiber 5.5g	**22%**
Sugars 8.9g	
Protein 11.7g	

Vitamin A 18%   •   Vitamin C 116%

Calcium 11%   •   Iron 21%

Nutrition Grade A

* Based on a 2000 calorie diet

Vitamix Ginger Carrot Soup

This is a simple ginger soup recipe that is very delicious and healthy and has simple ingredients that work well together.

Ingredients:

- 1 yellow onion, diced
- 1 1 lb. bag of baby carrots
- 1 tbsp. olive oil
- 1 tsp. salt
- 2 tbsp. ginger, chopped fresh
- 4 cups vegetable broth

Directions:

1. Heat oil in a Dutch oven or saucepan on medium.
2. Add onion and sauté for 6 minutes.

3. Add ginger, salt, broth and carrots and bring to a boil on high.
4. Reduce heat, cover and simmer for 20 minutes until carrots can be pierced with a fork easily.
5. Ladle or pour soup into Vitamix carefully, select Puree setting and puree until smooth.
6. Spoon into bowls and serve.

Servings: 4
Calories per Serving: 126

Nutrition Facts

Serving Size 376 g

Amount Per Serving

Calories 126   Calories from Fat 46

% **Daily Value***

Total Fat 5.1g	**8%**
Saturated Fat 0.9g	**5%**
Cholesterol 0mg	**0%**
Sodium 1393mg	**58%**
Potassium 540mg	**15%**
Total Carbohydrates 14.7g	**5%**
Dietary Fiber 4.2g	**17%**
Sugars 7.3g	
Protein 5.9g	

Vitamin A 313%   •   Vitamin C 8%

Calcium 6%   •   Iron 10%

Nutrition Grade A

* Based on a 2000 calorie diet

Vitamix Artichoke Cream Soup

This artichoke cream soup is very delicious and can be ready in just minutes, and it includes delicious macadamia nuts.

Ingredients:

- 2 tbsp. olive oil
- 4 cups vegetable broth
- ½ tsp. salt
- 4 cups frozen artichoke hearts, thawed
- 2 tbsp. garlic, minced
- ¼ cup raw macadamia nuts
- 2 onions, chopped
- 2 potatoes, peeled and diced
- 4 tbsp. chives, chopped
- Pepper to taste

Directions:

1. Heat oil on medium heat in a Dutch oven or a large soup pot.
2. Add garlic and onion and salt and sauté for 6 minutes.
3. And potatoes and sauté for another 10 minutes.
4. Add vegetable broth and artichokes and bring to a boil.
5. Reduce to simmer, cover and cook for 20 minutes until vegetables are tender.

6. Add macadamia nuts and ladle into Vitamix, select Setting 1.
7. Slowly increase speed to 10 and then High.
8. Blend 3-4 minutes or longer until mixture is fully pureed.
9. Add into bowls, season with pepper and chives and serve.

Servings: 8
Calories per Serving: 169

Nutrition Facts

Serving Size 294 g

Amount Per Serving

Calories 169   Calories from Fat 68

% Daily Value*

Total Fat 7.6g	**12%**
Saturated Fat 1.2g	**6%**
Cholesterol 0mg	**0%**
Sodium 610mg	**25%**
Potassium 688mg	**20%**
Total Carbohydrates 21.3g	**7%**
Dietary Fiber 6.7g	**27%**
Sugars 3.2g	
Protein 6.8g	

Vitamin A 2%	•	Vitamin C 39%
Calcium 6%	•	Iron 10%

Nutrition Grade A

* Based on a 2000 calorie diet

Vitamix Vegetable Chowder

This is a perfect vegetable chowder that doesn't take much time to make and is a great holiday dish or a small meal.

Ingredients:

- 2 cloves garlic, quartered
- 1 tbsp. butter
- ½ onion, chopped
- 2 cups vegetable broth
- 2 cups corn kernels, frozen

- ½ tsp. chili powder
- ¼ tsp. white pepper
- ¼ tsp. sea salt
- 1 cup red potatoes
- 1 cup carrot coins, frozen
- Salt and pepper to taste

Directions:

1. Heat oven to 450 degrees and coat potatoes with salt and pepper.
2. Wrap potatoes in foil and bake for 60 minutes.
3. Cut potatoes in half and check for doneness (some may need more time).
4. Heat butter in a large saucepan on medium
5. Add onion and garlic and sauté about 6 minutes.
6. Add vegetable broth, white pepper, salt, corn and chili powder and bring to a boil.
7. Reduce heat to low and simmer uncovered for 10 minutes.
8. Ladle soup into Vitamix blender and add potato.
9. Select Puree select Setting 1.
10. Slowly increase speed to 10 and then High.
11. Blend 3-4 minutes or longer until mixture is fully pureed.
12. Transfer back into saucepan and add carrots
13. Heat soup until carrots are tender.
14. Ladle into bowls and serve.

Servings: 8
Calories per Serving: 77

Nutrition Facts

Serving Size 141 g

Amount Per Serving

Calories 77 | Calories from Fat 19

% Daily Value*

Total Fat 2.1g	**3%**
Saturated Fat 1.1g	**5%**
Trans Fat 0.0g	
Cholesterol 4mg	**1%**
Sodium 273mg	**11%**
Potassium 288mg	**8%**
Total Carbohydrates 13.1g	**4%**
Dietary Fiber 1.8g	**7%**
Sugars 2.5g	
Protein 2.8g	

Vitamin A 48%	•	Vitamin C 9%
Calcium 1%	•	Iron 8%

Nutrition Grade A

* Based on a 2000 calorie diet

Vitamix Broccoli Cheddar Soup

This is an easy low calorie cheddar broccoli soup if you prefer cheddar cheese in your broccoli soup but don't want all the extra calories that come with it.

Ingredients:

- 1 cup water
- ¼ tsp. salt
- ¼ tsp. black pepper
- ¼ tsp. nutmeg
- 1 cup vegetable broth
- 3 ounces cheddar cheese
- 4 cups broccoli florets, steamed

Directions:

1. Steam broccoli florets in a vegetable steamer or in a saucepan.
2. Add half of ingredients, broth and water and broccoli into Vitamix blender and blend on setting 7 for about 3 minutes.
3. Pour into saucepan, add remaining half of ingredients, broth, water and broccoli and blend on 7 for about 3 minutes.
4. Ladle into bowls and serve.

Servings: 4
Calories per Serving: 127

Nutrition Facts

Serving Size 232 g

Amount Per Serving

Calories 127   Calories from Fat 70

	% Daily Value*
Total Fat 7.7g	**12%**
Saturated Fat 4.6g	**23%**
Trans Fat 0.0g	
Cholesterol 22mg	**7%**
Sodium 502mg	**21%**
Potassium 363mg	**10%**
Total Carbohydrates 6.7g	**2%**
Dietary Fiber 2.4g	**10%**
Sugars 1.9g	
Protein 9.1g	

Vitamin A 16%	•	Vitamin C 135%
Calcium 20%	•	Iron 5%

Nutrition Grade A-

* Based on a 2000 calorie diet

Vitamix Tomato Basil Soup

This is another simple tomato soup that includes basil for a different taste than the other tomato soup recipe in this book.

Ingredients:

- 4 cups tomatoes, diced
- 3 cups tomato juice
- 2 tbsp. butter
- 1 cup chicken broth
- 12 basil leaves
- ½ cup half and half

Directions:

1. Heat butter in a large saucepan until it starts to brown.
2. Add 2 cups of tomato juice and broth.
3. Add tomatoes, basil and tomato juice into Vitamix blender and select Setting 1.
4. Slowly increase speed to 10 and then High.
5. Blend 3-4 minutes or longer until mixture is fully pureed.
6. Add blended mixture into saucepan, cover and simmer for 20 minutes.
7. Remove from heat and allow to cool slightly.
8. Add half and half and stir and serve.

Servings: 4
Calories per Serving: 164

Nutrition Facts

Serving Size 461 g

Amount Per Serving

Calories 164   Calories from Fat 90

% **Daily Value***

Total Fat 10.0g	**15%**
Saturated Fat 6.0g	**30%**
Cholesterol 26mg	**9%**
Sodium 743mg	**31%**
Potassium 941mg	**27%**
Total Carbohydrates 16.3g	**5%**
Dietary Fiber 2.9g	**12%**
Sugars 11.4g	
Protein 5.2g	

Vitamin A 54%	•	Vitamin C 98%
Calcium 7%	•	Iron 8%

Nutrition Grade A-

* Based on a 2000 calorie diet

Vitamix Spinach Soup

If you love spinach this is a quick recipe for a nice spinach soup that takes just 20 minutes to make in total include prep time.

Ingredients:

- 1 onion, chopped
- 1 tsp. tarragon, dried
- 3 garlic cloves, crushed
- 1 lb. chopped frozen spinach, defrosted
- 2 tbsp. butter
- 6 cups chicken or vegetable stock

Directions:

1. Add butter into a large saucepan and heat on medium.
2. Add garlic and onions and sauté for 6 minutes.
3. Add chicken stock and bring to a boil.
4. Add spinach and tarragon.
5. Reduce heat to low, cover and simmer for 20 minutes.
6. Remove from heat, ladle into Vitamix blender select Puree select Setting 1.
7. Slowly increase speed to 10 and then High.
8. Blend 3-4 minutes or longer until mixture is fully pureed.
9. Portion into bowls and serve.

Servings: 8
Calories per Serving: 204

Nutrition Facts

Serving Size 180 g

Amount Per Serving

Calories 204   Calories from Fat 57

% Daily Value*

Total Fat 6.3g	**10%**
Saturated Fat 2.8g	**14%**
Trans Fat 0.0g	
Cholesterol 88mg	**29%**
Sodium 132mg	**6%**
Potassium 541mg	**15%**
Total Carbohydrates 3.8g	**1%**
Dietary Fiber 1.6g	**6%**
Sugars 0.8g	
Protein 32.3g	

Vitamin A 109%   •   Vitamin C 29%

Calcium 8%   •   Iron 14%

Nutrition Grade A

* Based on a 2000 calorie diet

Vitamix Bacon Cheddar Soup

If you love bacon this is a great bacon and cheddar soup that isn't the healthiest but is definitely delicious and easy to make.

Ingredients:

- ½ tsp. salt
- 3 ounces bacon, crumbled and cooked
- 2 cups low fat milk
- ½ tsp. rosemary
- ½ tsp. dill weed
- 2 russet potatoes, baked
- 1/3 cup cheddar cheese, shredded
- ¼ onion, chopped
- 1 tbsp. olive oil

Directions:

1. Wrap russet potatoes in foil and bake in oven at 450F for 60 minutes.
2. Sauté onion in olive oil on medium in a saucepan for 6 minutes.
3. Add milk, one potato, onion, dill weed, cheese, salt and rosemary into Vitamix and select Setting 1.
4. Slowly increase speed to 10 and then High.
5. Blend 5 minutes then reduce speed.
6. Remove lid and add remaining potato and bacon
7. Blend another 15 seconds until chopped.

Servings: 4
Calories per Serving: 273

Nutrition Facts

Serving Size 264 g

Amount Per Serving

Calories 273   Calories from Fat 125

% Daily Value*

Total Fat 13.9g	**21%**
Saturated Fat 5.2g	**26%**
Trans Fat 0.0g	
Cholesterol 32mg	**11%**
Sodium 737mg	**31%**
Potassium 722mg	**21%**
Total Carbohydrates 24.0g	**8%**
Dietary Fiber 2.8g	**11%**
Sugars 7.9g	
Protein 13.6g	

Vitamin A 7%	•	Vitamin C 36%
Calcium 23%	•	Iron 5%

Nutrition Grade B

* Based on a 2000 calorie diet

Vitamix Potato Celery Soup

This is a simple potato celery soup that takes about 45 minutes to make but is well worth the time.

Ingredients:

- 1 pound celery, chopped
- 2 medium onions, chopped
- 1 cup low fat milk
- 2 Russet potatoes, quartered and baked
- 4 garlic cloves, peeled and crushed
- 3 tbsp. olive oil
- 2 ½ cups vegetable stock

Directions:

1. Wrap Russet potatoes in foil and bake in oven at 450F for 60 minutes. Remove and quarter.
2. Sauté onions, garlic and celery in a Dutch oven or large saucepan on medium with olive oil for about 7 minutes or until softened.
3. Add potatoes, salt, garlic, low fat milk, onions and celery and garlic into Vitamix blender.
4. Slowly increase speed to 10 and blend for about 2 minutes.
5. Pour into bowls and serve.

Servings: 4
Calories per Serving: 233

Nutrition Facts

Serving Size 350 g

Amount Per Serving

Calories 233 | Calories from Fat 103

% **Daily Value***

Total Fat 11.4g	**18%**
Saturated Fat 1.9g	**10%**
Trans Fat 0.0g	
Cholesterol 2mg	**1%**
Sodium 164mg	**7%**
Potassium 913mg	**26%**
Total Carbohydrates 29.2g	**10%**
Dietary Fiber 5.6g	**22%**
Sugars 8.0g	
Protein 5.4g	

Vitamin A 11%	•	Vitamin C 50%
Calcium 14%	•	Iron 5%

Nutrition Grade A-

* Based on a 2000 calorie diet

Vitamix Creamy Carrot Soup

This is an easy creamy carrot soup that includes delicious onion and healthy olive oil.

Ingredients:

- 2 tbsp. chives, chopped
- 2 tsp. olive oil
- 4 cups chicken stock or vegetable stock
- 1 onion, chopped
- 1 cup short grain rice
- 1 carrot, sliced thinly
- Salt and pepper to taste

Directions:

1. Heat oil in large saucepan or Dutch oven on medium high.

2. Add onion and cook for 6 minutes.
3. Add carrots and cook another 2 minutes or so.
4. Add broth and rice and season with salt and pepper to taste.
5. Increase heat to boil and reduce to simmer.
6. Simmer about 30 minutes or until carrots are tender.
7. Ladle soup into Vitamix blender and use puree setting until smooth.
8. Scrape sides and puree again.
9. Add soup back into pan.
10. Season again with pepper and salt.
11. Garnish with chives and serve

Servings: 4
Calories per Serving: 228

Nutrition Facts

Serving Size 342 g

Amount Per Serving

Calories 228   Calories from Fat 26

% Daily Value*

Total Fat 2.9g	**5%**
Trans Fat 0.0g	
Cholesterol 0mg	**0%**
Sodium 775mg	**32%**
Potassium 108mg	**3%**
Total Carbohydrates 46.9g	**16%**
Dietary Fiber 1.0g	**4%**
Sugars 2.7g	
Protein 4.2g	

Vitamin A 52%	•	Vitamin C 6%
Calcium 3%	•	Iron 1%

Nutrition Grade C+

* Based on a 2000 calorie diet

Vitamix Asparagus Cream Soup

If you love asparagus this recipe is for you, and it is a delicious and simple cream of asparagus soup that is loaded with asparagus.

Ingredients:

- ¼ onion, chopped
- 1 12 oz. package frozen asparagus or 1 lb. fresh asparagus
- 1 ½ cups chicken broth
- 1 cup of low fat milk

Directions:

1. Cut coarse ends of asparagus if you are using fresh asparagus.

2. Add 2 cups of water to a saucepan and cook asparagus on medium high in boiling water, about 6 minutes.
3. Drain the water and reserve 1 cup.
4. Cut tips off asparagus, chop and reserve.
5. Add onion, chicken stock and reserved asparagus water into another pan and increase heat to boil.
6. Add chopped asparagus and reduce heat to low and simmer uncovered for 5 minutes.
7. Ladle mixture into Vitamix blender select Setting 1.
8. Slowly increase speed to 10 and then High.
9. Blend 3-4 minutes or longer until mixture is fully pureed.
10. Return blended mixture into saucepan and add milk and reheat for 3 minutes while stirring.
11. Season with salt and pepper as desired and serve.

Servings: 4
Calories per Serving: 65

Nutrition Facts

Serving Size 243 g

Amount Per Serving

Calories 65   Calories from Fat 17

	% Daily Value*
Total Fat 1.9g	**3%**
Saturated Fat 0.9g	**5%**
Cholesterol 5mg	**2%**
Sodium 317mg	**13%**
Potassium 294mg	**8%**
Total Carbohydrates 7.3g	**2%**
Dietary Fiber 1.9g	**8%**
Sugars 4.9g	
Protein 5.8g	

Vitamin A 13%	•	Vitamin C 9%
Calcium 10%	•	Iron 11%

Nutrition Grade A

* Based on a 2000 calorie diet

Vitamix Tomato and Swiss Soup

This is a unique soup that includes healthy Swiss chard and tomato and can be ready in about 30 minutes.

Ingredients:

- 1 cup low fat milk
- 1 onion, chopped
- 4 cups chicken stock
- 1 bunch of Swiss chard, chopped (separate stems and leaves)
- 2 tbsp. butter
- 2 Yukon gold potatoes, diced and peeled
- Salt and pepper to taste
- Cilantro for garnish

Directions:

1. Add butter in a large saucepan on medium heat.
2. Add Swiss chard stems and onions and sauté for 5 minutes or until softened.
3. Add milk, potatoes, and chicken stock and bring to boil.
4. Simmer for 6 minutes or until potatoes are soft.
5. Add Swiss chard leaves and simmer another 6 minutes.
6. Add soup into Vitamix blender with a ladle and puree until smooth.
7. Add to soup bowls, garnish with cilantro and serve.

Servings: 4
Calories per Serving: 177

Nutrition Facts

Serving Size 480 g

Amount Per Serving

Calories 177　　　　　　Calories from Fat 71

% Daily Value*

Total Fat 7.9g	**12%**
Saturated Fat 4.6g	**23%**
Trans Fat 0.0g	
Cholesterol 20mg	**7%**
Sodium 959mg	**40%**
Potassium 659mg	**19%**
Total Carbohydrates 23.5g	**8%**
Dietary Fiber 2.7g	**11%**
Sugars 5.8g	
Protein 5.8g	

Vitamin A 70%	•	Vitamin C 57%
Calcium 13%	•	Iron 10%

Nutrition Grade B+

* Based on a 2000 calorie diet

Vitamix Sweet Potato and Macadamia Soup

This is an easy and delicious sweet potato soup that is a great alternative to some of the soups that use regular potatoes.

Ingredients:

- ½ cup raw macadamia nuts
- 2 red onions, cut into quarters
- 3 tbsp. olive oil

- 4 lbs. sweet potato, peeled and cut into chunks
- 8 cups vegetable stock
- A handful of chopped macadamia nuts for garnish
- Cilantro for garnish
- Salt to taste

Directions:

1. Toss sweet potato and onion in olive oil and salt to taste.
2. Roast at 325 F on a baking dish for about 50 minutes to 1 hour, check to make sure it isn't burning.
3. Add vegetable stock to a large saucepan and add roasted sweet potato and onion.
4. Simmer for 12 minutes.
5. Allow to cool, add macadamia nuts, and ladle into Vitamix and puree until smooth.
6. Add pureed soup back to saucepan and simmer 2-3 minutes.
7. Garnish with cilantro and chopped macadamia nuts and serve.

Servings: 8
Calories per Serving: 321

Nutrition Facts

Serving Size 268 g

Amount Per Serving

Calories 321   Calories from Fat 108

% Daily Value*

Total Fat 12.0g	**19%**
Saturated Fat 1.8g	**9%**
Cholesterol 0mg	**0%**
Sodium 102mg	**4%**
Potassium 1148mg	**33%**
Total Carbohydrates 50.7g	**17%**
Dietary Fiber 8.9g	**35%**
Sugars 16.3g	
Protein 5.5g	

Vitamin A 17%	•	Vitamin C 126%
Calcium 2%	•	Iron 46%

Nutrition Grade A

* Based on a 2000 calorie diet

Vitamix Potato and Garlic Soup

This is a very hearty and rustic potato and garlic soup that can warm you up on a cold day and is very easy to make.

Ingredients:

- 8 cups vegetable broth
- 2 red onions, chopped roughly
- 2 tbsp. olive oil
- 6 red potatoes, sliced and washed
- 2 full heads of garlic
- Parsley for garnish
- Salt and pepper to taste

Directions:

1. Preheat oven to 400 F.
2. Add unpeeled garlic cloves to a baking tray and roast for 30 minutes. Remove and set aside.
3. Cook potatoes in boiling water for 12 minutes.
4. Sauté onions in a large saucepan with 2 tbsp. olive oil on medium for about 18 minutes or until caramelized.
5. Add vegetable broth, bring to boil and simmer.
6. Add potatoes after draining them.
7. Peel garlic and add into soup and season with salt and pepper to taste.
8. Simmer for 14 minutes until potatoes are tender.
9. Pulse for a few seconds in Vitamix blender by setting speed to 1 and chopping for about 30 seconds – just enough to chop ingredients roughly.
10. Portion into bowls and serve.

Servings: 8
Calories per Serving: 200

Nutrition Facts

Serving Size 437 g

Amount Per Serving

Calories 200 | Calories from Fat 46

% Daily Value*

Total Fat 5.2g	**8%**
Saturated Fat 0.9g	**5%**
Cholesterol 0mg	**0%**
Sodium 775mg	**32%**
Potassium 996mg	**28%**
Total Carbohydrates 30.8g	**10%**
Dietary Fiber 3.4g	**14%**
Sugars 3.5g	
Protein 8.5g	

Vitamin A 0% • Vitamin C 29%

Calcium 4% • Iron 10%

Nutrition Grade A-

* Based on a 2000 calorie diet

Vitamix Green Pea Soup

This green pea soup is a delicious option that includes potatoes, lettuce, and other delicious ingredients.

Ingredients:

- 6 cups green peas, frozen
- 3 tbsp. lemon juice
- 3 cloves garlic, chopped
- 1 cup fresh mint leaves
- 4 cups vegetable stock
- 2 tbsp. olive oil
- 2 large red potatoes, peeled and diced
- 1 head of lettuce (Iceberg), shredded
- Salt and pepper to taste

Directions:

1. Sauté onions and garlic and salt and pepper in olive oil on medium heat in a large saucepan until soft, about 6 minutes.
2. Add lettuce and cook until wilted.
3. Add peas and mix.
4. Add vegetable stock and bring to a boil.
5. Cover and simmer until peas are tender, about 14-16 minutes.
6. Allow to cool slightly, add to Vitamix with ladle, select puree setting then puree in Vitamix until smooth. Repeat if needed.
7. Add back into pot and season with lemon juice and salt and pepper and mint to taste.

8. Serve immediately.

Servings: 8
Calories per Serving: 215

Nutrition Facts

Serving Size 384 g

Amount Per Serving

Calories 215   Calories from Fat 45

% Daily Value*

Total Fat 5.0g	**8%**
Saturated Fat 0.9g	**4%**
Cholesterol 0mg	**0%**
Sodium 400mg	**17%**
Potassium 909mg	**26%**
Total Carbohydrates 33.5g	**11%**
Dietary Fiber 8.2g	**33%**
Sugars 8.0g	
Protein 10.7g	

Vitamin A 26%   •   Vitamin C 96%
Calcium 7%   •   Iron 28%

Nutrition Grade A

* Based on a 2000 calorie diet

Vitamix Pumpkin Soup

Any good soup recipe book has at least one pumpkin soup recipe, and here is a very easy and delicious one that is quite simple to make.

Ingredients:

- ½ tsp. nutmeg
- 1 cup vegetable broth
- ½ onion, sliced
- 1 ½ cups pumpkin, canned
- ¼ cup coconut milk, unsweetened
- 2 garlic cloves, crushed and peeled
- 1 ½ tbsp. brown sugar
- ½ tsp. paprika
- 1 tbsp. olive oil
- Salt and pepper to taste

Directions:

1. Sauté onions and garlic in 1 tbsp. of olive oil in a large saucepan.
2. Add all ingredients to saucepan, season with salt and pepper to taste, and bring to a simmer for 5 minutes.
3. Add all ingredients into Vitamix and start at speed 1, gradually increasing to speed 10 and finally High.
4. Blend for about 7 minutes.
5. Portion into bowls and serve.

Servings: 4
Calories per Serving: 64

Nutrition Facts

Serving Size 95 g

Amount Per Serving

Calories 64   Calories from Fat 35

% Daily Value*

Total Fat 3.9g	**6%**
Saturated Fat 2.0g	**10%**
Cholesterol 0mg	**0%**
Sodium 100mg	**4%**
Potassium 159mg	**5%**
Total Carbohydrates 7.0g	**2%**
Dietary Fiber 1.8g	**7%**
Sugars 3.8g	
Protein 1.4g	

Vitamin A 144%   •   Vitamin C 5%

Calcium 2%   •   Iron 5%

Nutrition Grade B+

* Based on a 2000 calorie diet

Vitamix Almond Broccoli Soup

This is a unique take on traditional broccoli soup and is flavored with almonds and zucchini.

Ingredients:

- 1 zucchini, steamed and sliced
- 1 cup almonds, roasted
- 3 cups vegetable stock
- 4 cups broccoli florets, steamed
- Salt and pepper to taste

Directions:

1. Steam vegetables for 10 minutes in a vegetable steamer basket.
2. Preheat oven to 350 F.
3. Add almonds to Vitamix blender and blend on setting 3 for a minute or two until almonds are coarsely chopped.
4. Add almond meal to cookie sheet and toast in oven for 7 minutes.
5. Remove 2 tbsp. of almonds to garnish soup.
6. Heat vegetable stock to a simmer.
7. Add stock to blender, followed by almonds broccoli florets, and zucchini.
8. Select Setting 1.
9. Slowly increase speed to 10 and then High.
10. Blend 3-4 minutes or longer until mixture is fully pureed.

11. Season with salt and pepper, garnish with almonds and serve.

Servings: 4
Calories per Serving: 205

Nutrition Facts

Serving Size 344 g

Amount Per Serving

Calories 205 | Calories from Fat 120

% Daily Value*

Total Fat 13.3g	**20%**
Saturated Fat 1.2g	**6%**
Trans Fat 0.0g	
Cholesterol 0mg	**0%**
Sodium 608mg	**25%**
Potassium 746mg	**21%**
Total Carbohydrates 13.5g	**4%**
Dietary Fiber 5.9g	**24%**
Sugars 3.9g	
Protein 11.8g	

Vitamin A 13%	•	Vitamin C 149%
Calcium 12%	•	Iron 12%

Nutrition Grade A

* Based on a 2000 calorie diet

Vitamix Gazpacho Soup

This is a simple and delicious gazpacho recipe that can be made in just about 10 minutes.

Ingredients:

- 1 onion, chopped finely
- 2 cups of water
- 1 Anaheim pepper, chopped finely
- 3 tbsp. bread crumbs
- 1 cucumber, chopped finely
- 3 tbsp. red wine vinegar
- 3 cloves garlic, peeled and crushed
- 2 tbsp. toasted almonds
- 2 lbs. ripe tomatoes, halved and seeded
- 3 tbsp. olive oil
- Salt and pepper to taste

Directions:

1. Save ¼ of the chopped cucumber, and ¼ onion for garnish.
2. Chop each ingredient finely and mix them together in Vitamix blender.
3. Add to Vitamix blender, start at Setting 1 and slowly increase speed to 10.
4. Blend ingredients until smooth, about 3 minutes.
5. Serve cold with onion and cucumber with garnish.

Servings: 4

Calories per Serving: 196

Nutrition Facts

Serving Size 481 g

Amount Per Serving

Calories 196   Calories from Fat 115

% Daily Value*

Total Fat 12.8g	**20%**
Saturated Fat 1.8g	**9%**
Trans Fat 0.0g	
Cholesterol 0mg	**0%**
Sodium 55mg	**2%**
Potassium 739mg	**21%**
Total Carbohydrates 19.3g	**6%**
Dietary Fiber 4.3g	**17%**
Sugars 8.9g	
Protein 4.2g	

Vitamin A 39%   •   Vitamin C 60%

Calcium 7%   •   Iron 7%

Nutrition Grade A

* Based on a 2000 calorie diet

Vitamix Cold Corn Chowder

This is a very quick recipe for a delicious corn chowder that can work as a main course or a side dish. Can be served warm or cold

Ingredients:

- 1 cup coconut water
- 1 yellow bell pepper, chopped and seeded
- 1 ½ tbsp. lemon juice
- 2 tbsp. cilantro, chopped
- 2 cloves garlic, minced
- ¼ onion, chopped
- ½ tsp sea salt
- 2 cups corn kernels, room temperature
- Cilantro for garnish

Directions:

1. Add ingredients into Vitamix, select Setting 1.
2. Slowly increase speed to 10 and then High.
3. Blend 3-4 minutes or longer until mixture is fully pureed.
4. Serve cold with cilantro garnish or serve warm by adding hot water into blender.

Servings: 4
Calories per Serving: 86

Nutrition Facts

Serving Size 147 g

Amount Per Serving

Calories 86 | Calories from Fat 6

% Daily Value*

Total Fat 0.7g	**1%**
Cholesterol 0mg	**0%**
Sodium 278mg	**12%**
Potassium 338mg	**10%**
Total Carbohydrates 18.0g	**6%**
Dietary Fiber 2.6g	**11%**
Sugars 6.3g	
Protein 2.5g	

Vitamin A 19% • Vitamin C 76%

Calcium 1% • Iron 12%

Nutrition Grade A

* Based on a 2000 calorie diet

Vitamix Blueberry Soup

This is a nice and easy blueberry soup that is very delicious and refreshing and takes just minutes to make.

Ingredients:

- 2 cups yogurt
- 1 tbsp. honey
- ½ tsp. cinnamon
- 1 cup frozen blueberries
- 2 cups orange juice

Directions:

1. Add ingredients except ½ of blueberries into Vitamix blender.
2. Select puree select Setting 1.
3. Slowly increase speed to 10 and then High.
4. Blend just 30-45 seconds or so until mixture is well pureed.

5. Add remaining ½ of blueberries.
6. Serve cold

Servings: 4
Calories per Serving: 181

Nutrition Facts

Serving Size 288 g

Amount Per Serving

Calories 181   Calories from Fat 17

	% Daily Value*
Total Fat 1.9g	3%
Saturated Fat 1.3g	6%
Trans Fat 0.0g	
Cholesterol 7mg	2%
Sodium 87mg	4%
Potassium 567mg	16%
Total Carbohydrates 31.3g	10%
Dietary Fiber 1.3g	5%
Sugars 26.9g	
Protein 8.1g	

Vitamin A 1%	•	Vitamin C 184%
Calcium 23%	•	Iron 12%

Nutrition Grade A
* Based on a 2000 calorie diet

Vitamix Avocado Soup

This cold avocado soup is very cream and delicious and takes just minutes to prepare.

Ingredients:

- 2 avocados, pitted and diced
- 1 tbsp. olive oil
- 2 tbsp. lime juice
- 2 cups chicken stock
- 1 cup cream
- ¼ tsp. nutmeg
- 2 tomatoes, diced and seeded
- 2 tbsp. shallots, chopped
- Salt and pepper to taste

Directions:

1. Add avocado and tomato into Vitamix blender.
2. Select Setting 1.
3. Slowly increase speed to 10 and then High.
4. Blend just 30-45 seconds or so until mixture is well pureed.
5. Add shallots to olive oil in a frying pan and sauté for 6 minutes on medium.
6. Whisk avocado, cream, chicken stock together in a bowl.
7. Add nutmeg and salt and pepper to taste.
8. Chill for 30 minutes and serve.

Servings: 4
Calories per Serving: 294

Nutrition Facts

Serving Size 308 g

Amount Per Serving

Calories 294 　　　　　　　Calories from Fat 242

% Daily Value*

Total Fat 26.9g	**41%**
Saturated Fat 6.8g	**34%**
Trans Fat 0.0g	
Cholesterol 11mg	**4%**
Sodium 411mg	**17%**
Potassium 680mg	**19%**
Total Carbohydrates 14.2g	**5%**
Dietary Fiber 7.5g	**30%**
Sugars 3.7g	
Protein 3.4g	

Vitamin A 16% 　　•　　 Vitamin C 31%

Calcium 4% 　　•　　 Iron 5%

Nutrition Grade B-

* Based on a 2000 calorie diet

Vitamix Cantaloupe Soup

This is a very delicious cantaloupe soup that includes lime and agave nectar and is refreshing on a hot day.

Ingredients:

- 3 basil leaves
- 2 tbsp. lime juice
- Zest of 1 lime
- 1 cantaloupe, cubed
- 1 tsp. honey or agave nectar
- ¼ tsp. ginger, powdered
- 3 tbsp. water
- ¼ cup yogurt

Directions:

1. Add all ingredients except water into Vitamix blender.
2. Start at Setting 1 and increase slowly to 10 and finally High and blend for about 3 minutes or until smooth.
3. Add water to achieve desired consistency.
4. Refrigerate for at least 1-2 hours and serve cold.

Servings: 4
Calories per Serving: 28

Nutrition Facts

Serving Size 63 g

Amount Per Serving

Calories 28   Calories from Fat 2

	% Daily Value*
Total Fat 0.3g	**0%**
Cholesterol 1mg	**0%**
Sodium 17mg	**1%**
Potassium 132mg	**4%**
Total Carbohydrates 5.4g	**2%**
Sugars 5.2g	
Protein 1.2g	

Vitamin A 24%	•	Vitamin C 21%
Calcium 3%	•	Iron 1%

Nutrition Grade A

* Based on a 2000 calorie diet

Vitamix Cucumber Soup

This cold cucumber soup is made with yogurt and can keep you cool on a hot summer day.

Ingredients:

- 1 cup low fat milk
- 1 cucumber, seeded and washed
- 3 tbsp. chives, chopped
- 2 tbsp. cilantro or parsley, chopped
- 3 tbsp. fresh mint, chopped
- ½ cup plain yogurt
- ½ cup sour cream
- Salt and pepper to taste

Directions:

1. Set aside 1 tbsp. of chives for garnish
2. Add the milk, cucumber and herbs into Vitamix.
3. Select Setting 1.
4. Slowly increase speed to 10 and then High.
5. Blend 1 minute or until mixture is fully pureed.
6. Add milk and sour cream and puree until smooth.
7. Remove and add to a large bowl.
8. Stir in yogurt and season with pepper and salt to taste.
9. Refrigerate for 30 minutes to 1 hour.
10. Garnish with chives and serve.

Servings: 4
Calories per Serving: 128

Nutrition Facts

Serving Size 203 g

Amount Per Serving

Calories 128   Calories from Fat 70

% Daily Value*

Total Fat 7.8g	**12%**
Saturated Fat 4.8g	**24%**
Trans Fat 0.0g	
Cholesterol 19mg	**6%**
Sodium 69mg	**3%**
Potassium 288mg	**8%**
Total Carbohydrates 9.6g	**3%**
Dietary Fiber 0.8g	**3%**
Sugars 6.3g	
Protein 5.4g	

Vitamin A 12%	•	Vitamin C 8%
Calcium 19%	•	Iron 5%

Nutrition Grade B

* Based on a 2000 calorie diet

Vitamix Nectarine Soup

This is an easy to make nectarine soup that is sweet and refreshing and includes lemon as well as grape juice.

Ingredients:

- 4 nectarines, pitted
- 1 cup white or red grape juice, cold
- 1/2 lemon, peeled
- 1 tbsp. honey or agave nectar
- ½ tsp. cinnamon
- ¼ cup yogurt
- Zest of 1 lemon
- Mint leaves for garnish

Directions:

1. Put ingredients in Vitamix and select Setting 1.
2. Increase slowly to Setting 10 and then to High.
3. Blend for about 1 minute or until smooth.
4. Remove to a large bowl and stir in yogurt.
5. Refrigerate for 30 minutes to 1 hour.
6. Garnish with lemon zest and mint leaves and serve.

Servings: 4
Calories per Serving: 114

Nutrition Facts

Serving Size 237 g

Amount Per Serving

Calories 114   Calories from Fat 6

	% Daily Value*
Total Fat 0.7g	**1%**
Trans Fat 0.0g	
Cholesterol 1mg	**0%**
Sodium 12mg	**0%**
Potassium 425mg	**12%**
Total Carbohydrates 26.3g	**9%**
Dietary Fiber 2.6g	**11%**
Sugars 22.2g	
Protein 2.7g	

Vitamin A 10%	•	Vitamin C 52%
Calcium 5%	•	Iron 3%

Nutrition Grade A

* Based on a 2000 calorie diet

Vitamix Lychee Mango Soup

If you haven't tried lychee fruit before this soup is the perfect recipe to give it a go, and it's also flavored with refreshing mango.

Ingredients:

- Juice of 1 lime
- Zest of 1 lime
- 30 lychees, seeded and peeled
- 3 tbsp. olive oil
- 1 mango, peeled and pitted
- 1.5 oz. candied ginger
- Mint for garnish

Directions:

1. Put ingredients in Vitamix and select Setting 1.
2. Increase slowly to Setting 10 and then to High.
3. Blend for about 1 minute or until smooth.
4. Refrigerate for 30 minutes to 1 hour.
5. Portion into bowls and add mint for garnish and serve.

Servings: 4
Calories per Serving: 180

Nutrition Facts

Serving Size 146 g

Amount Per Serving

Calories 180   Calories from Fat 100

	% Daily Value*
Total Fat 11.1g	**17%**
Saturated Fat 1.6g	**8%**
Cholesterol 0mg	**0%**
Sodium 2mg	**0%**
Potassium 232mg	**7%**
Total Carbohydrates 21.9g	**7%**
Dietary Fiber 2.0g	**8%**
Sugars 18.9g	
Protein 1.0g	

Vitamin A 8%	•	Vitamin C 111%
Calcium 1%	•	Iron 3%

Nutrition Grade B-

* Based on a 2000 calorie diet

Conclusion

The Vitamix is one of the highest quality and most versatile blenders available anywhere, and using it to make soups will hopefully give you much more utility out of your blender. The quality of soup purees that the Vitamix blender can make is amazingly good, and the blender takes a much shorter amount of time to blend ingredients than many other blenders on the market because of its high power.

As you probably have seen from the nutrition information, most of these recipes are very low calorie and can be a great option for meals on a weight loss diet. Sometimes smoothies can be overloaded with carbohydrates and sugar, and soups can make a great alternative meal to smoothies because they usually don't have as many carbohydrates like the soups in this book. We were careful to pick recipes that are not very calorie rich, and even the recipes that use rich ingredients like butter only use small quantities of them.

There are three main series for Vitamix blenders, the S-Series, C-Series, and G-Series, and this recipe book will work for any of the blender models from these series. All of the blenders are virtually the same and are made with the same high quality materials; there are only a few differences between them such as supplementary DVDs, dishwasher save containers, and program settings. You can't really go wrong no matter which Vitamix model that you use for these recipes.

These recipes can be easily scaled up or down as needed, and many of them yield 4 to 8 servings. Remember to use caution when moving the hot soup to and from the blender, and the Vitamix comes with a built in steam escape specifically for the purpose of blending hot soups safely, so don't be alarmed if you see steam venting out of your blender.

Remember that the Vitamix itself will actually heat up your soups from the friction of the blades, so you need to be careful when making some of the cold soups and don't blend the ingredients for too long, but if you do blend for a longer amount of time be sure to refrigerate before serving. If you are having trouble with a cold soup being too warm feel free to add ice to the ingredient.

The hot soups can be ladled into the Vitamix when they are cooled down for your safely and they will heat up once the blender gets running for at least 2 to 4 minutes on high, and it will heat the soup up by several degrees.

We hope you enjoy these Vitamix soup recipes and that they inspire you to be creative with your blender and find out many other new ways to use it, and feel free to adjust the ingredients, as you prefer. For example, parsley can be substituted for cilantro in many of these recipes and vice versa, and vegetable stock can be substituted for chicken stock for vegans and vegetarians.

Photos Courtesy of freedigitalphotos.net and their respective creators

14703454R00050

Printed in Great Britain
by Amazon.co.uk, Ltd.,
Marston Gate.